From Lilith to Mary

An Inspirational Journey from Alcoholism to Recovery

Tai Alonna Batov

SPIRAL LIGHT

PERSONAL
DEVELOPMENT

Spiral Light Personal Development

Contents

Description

A redemptive story of healing and transformation, this is an autobiographical short. This story is being shared to inspire people to take responsibility for what they can (their choices and decisions), to make a path for a better life. For me, living my best life means that I can be of maximum service to my creator God. That I'm not bogged down by egotism, fear, trauma consciousness, economic scarcity, or anything other thing that sucks my attention and reduces my effectiveness to serve God with my highest potential.

Dedication

This book is dedicated to my family- all of whom have seen the absolute worst and shining best in me. I am so grateful for your endless love.

Prologue

I know that some people will read this book and not believe or understand it. That is OKAY. It's my story. MINE. I own it. I take responsibility for it. And I'm writing it for people who need inspiration to find the courage to take a healing path. Prior to sobriety, I would have cared. A LOT. About what people thought of me. Caring superficially or deeply about others' opinions of me, good or bad, defeats the purpose and progress in healing. So I simply don't do it. It's something that you can train yourself out of. As a matter of fact, we humans are so smart that we can train ourselves out of any self-destructive pattern or behavior.

Really, this is intended to help folks move from keeping themselves small to magnetizing their highest potential. It is for the specific group of people who knowingly or unknowingly operate out of a base of fear; fear of change, fear of success, fear of failure. Women whose divine birthright of self-worth has been replaced with doubt, shame, and guilt.

Judgers and haters — it's okay, come forth, — you are here because you need healing too. Also it's important to note that those whom I shared my first three drinks with are completely innocent. They are wonderful people for whom I have deep love and affection. There is no way they could have possibly known I was born alcoholic.

This is not a manual. In my humble opinion, there does not exist a "how to" for healing. Healing is not a formulated act; it is an unpredictable combination of events that leads one slowly or spontaneously to make choices that catalyze healing. The formulaic aspect is 1. recognizing that healing needs to take place and 2. making room for it. Awareness + Willingness + Action = Potential for Healing. In other words, you have to really want it! The humility that is required to admit imperfection and the need for help can generally be a catalyst for transformational change.

There is a limited depth to which I will write about my drinking experiences, because this isn't meant to be one long drunkalog. It's meant to be an inspiration, to encourage women who have stunted their growth due to the shame of events surrounding alcohol. In truth, I have a deep respect for the two children my husband and I are blessed to raise. I'm conscious that it would be unfair to burden their hearts with information that would cause them embarrassment and trigger shame for them. Of all the things I wish to pass to those kind and thoughtful kids, my past trauma is off of the list.

Chapter One

CALIFORNIA; BEYOND AND BACK

My first drink — I am five years old and it is 1981. My babysitters, a small group of giggling beautiful young women are close family friends. They are approximately 13 years older than me. There is a game of quarters happening, centered around a red plastic solo cup. A vivid recollection doesn't exist, but I remember gasps of delight as my quarter bounced in. A sip of beer. And nausea. A terrible feeling sits inside my stomach, and everything is swirling. I feel awful and don't remember the rest.

My second drink — I'm approximately 11 years old. It is a glass of chardonnay at Christmas with mom and her close friend in Vacaville. My mom, brother, and I moved there when I was in 5th grade. Moving was difficult, but the diverse larger town with two high schools was a welcome change from the racist prison town of 7,000 that staged our family's early beginning. My mom and her friend are barely able to hold back snorts of laughter as they were watching me slur my words, unable to put together a complete sentence in front of the roaring fireplace.

The third, and what I now think should have been the last drink of my life, happens at 14 years old. Me and my middle school bestie snuck out by taxi (I still can't fathom that a taxi picked us up without parental consent in 1991 — or where we got the money for it!). We are drinking whiskey behind a church in town with two older boys. Blackout. Agonizing nausea and waves of sickness rise from my stomach to my throat as I come to inside her bedroom in the morning. It never occurred to me, over all these years, that I wasn't worried about not remembering how we got to her home or distraught about the sickened state of my body. I believe that most people would categorize that experience as abnormal or adverse. Being allergic to alcohol, however, I came to relive that moment many, many times in my life.

The Circus — Discovery of vodka!

While all of my high school friends were in college and university in the mid-1990's, I was in the circus. The Ringling Brothers Barnum and Bailey Circus. At the time of this writing, other than childbirth, that has been the single most formative experience of my life. High school graduation at 16 was nothing spectacular. After my freshman year in high school, I had started cutting school and experimented with cigarettes. My mom was a single mom who worked outside of the home, and my brother was five years older than me, and our home life wasn't super close knit. Mom took me to my dance classes in a neighboring town 15 minutes away, and I was on the drill team — but by the time I reached my junior year, I was a bit of a mess. One time during my sophomore year, I had a party at my house when my mom was out of town. (My brother had already moved away to Europe, so there was no supervision). I cleaned up everything as if there had been a crime scene that needed to be wiped of prints. But my major failure was not throwing all of the garbage bags away, and my parole agent mom spied one in the garage. She went digging, and I was grounded for a month. In retrospect, I was naturally bright as a young girl, so it's interesting that I didn't take the final step to rid our home of evidence that I'd broken the rules. I suspect there was an element of wanting to get caught, a cry for help. It was during this party, at the age of 13, I gave up my virginity to someone I wasn't even dating and didn't even really like that much. I just thought it was cool that we shared the same rare[1] birthday. In the ensuing semesters, my internal identity crisis became full blown. On the outside, I was nice, pretty, and liked. On the inside, I felt insecure, confused, and not grounded.

At that point, my mom was frustrated and overwhelmed that I wouldn't simply click in and do what I was being told to do, so she offered an unorthodox solution. I could live by myself in a townhouse that she bought in Sacramento, 45 minutes away, and attend a performing arts high school. Looking back, I have nothing but love and compassion for my mom. She was an unsupported single parent who waged her bets that I would step up into independence. And partly, she was right. I picked up self-sufficiency skills at 15 years old that would blow navy seals out of the water. The sharper side of that double edge sword, however, was fully attaching to a rejection wound that began with my father leaving at the age of three, and never becoming an integral part of my childhood. The wound got bigger and festered with time and experience.

---

1. *Christmas Day

In September of 1994, I was 16 and had graduated high school three months previously. Other than dance, my life was boring, and I didn't have a lot of friends locally. (Remember I spent most of my high school in another town). I felt somewhat disconnected, like life was happening inside a glass building, and I was on the outside looking in. I was in city college, taking six classes, earning all A's and one B. I had already botched my chance of getting a cruise ship gig. I actually think the Universe botched it for me because there was someplace else I was meant to be! I remember getting ready for a Broadway dance review with the local dance company I was a part of. My mom had cut a two-line advertisement out of the local paper sharing an audition for dancer showgirls for Ringling Brothers and Barnum and Bailey Circus. I looked at it and shrugged my shoulders. "It's on Thursday night. I'm not in the cast performing on Thursday night; I'll go." As I walked into what was then known as Arco Arena, a feeling came over me. I KNEW, like I KNEW, like I KNEW, that was where I was meant to be. Fate. Destiny. Kismet. Something inside my soul KNEW that I belonged there. Eyeing the dancers on the Spanish Web, my heart leapt with excitement.

This is the part of this little book, where you are convinced beyond a shadow of a doubt that *if something is meant for you, it will happen.*

After my audition, I was immediately offered a contract verbally, and given direction that my contract would be mailed to me. All dancers were to sign it immediately and return it. I spent the next two months over the moon. Everything was completed with an amplified excitement; withdrawing from college classes, going through my paperwork, and figuring out what to bring with me for my new life on the road. As October started to wind down, I felt nervous and got a pinch in my stomach when I thought about my contract. Where was it? Why hadn't I received it? What if the new life I had already emotionally put myself into didn't come to pass, and I got stuck?

In those pre-internet days, people had access to national yellow pages. I looked up Ringling Bros. in Vienna, VA. I dialed the number and asked for HR. (I don't know how I knew how to do that). After a short series of transfers, I explained to the woman on the other end of the line who I was and why I was calling. She responded. "Well, it's a good thing you called when you did! In one more hour, I was preparing to send your contract out to another dancer. We sent two contracts to you with no response." Come to find out Fed-Ex couldn't figure out how to deliver it to my town home, 26 Park Place. That was my second conscious experience with divine intervention.

Manhattan 1999

She screamed into the phone, "What do you mean you are moving to New York? What day do you arrive?" With excited confidence, I said the date, to my recollection it was in August. My dear friend that I had met in the circus was the first person I called when I arrived in New York, living at my brother's apartment in Manhattan. She replied that we were going out that night. And so, that night led to the beginning of many more that ended in utter oblivion.

Of course, when one is in their late teens and early 20's, especially in previous decades that didn't boast sobriety as sexy, it was normal and expected to feel immortal while young. My boyfriend from the circus was a performing artist, touring the United States on contract. So it was me and my girlfriends. Being young, taking crazy risks, being drunk — it wasn't illegal. Hangovers in Manhattan were common — fueled by taxis and dangerous subway rides, it was so easy to slide by in life being very drunk very often. Making it to work everyday and engaging in art and culture masked my alcoholism. Alcoholism, which I had dipped my toe into, unbeknownst to me. A big factor in not understanding that I was beset with a disease was a total and complete lack of education. I thought that a person with alcohol problems was toothless, unemployed, and lived outside under a bridge. That's it! I had no possible conception that it could look any other way.

After a particularly gnarly night out with my girlfriends — well, early morning to be exact — I contemplated a series of incredibly stupid and shameful decisions I had made. In an emotional knee jerk, I phoned one of the ladies that was in our party the night before. One of the parts of the evening I did remember was her saying that she didn't drink alcohol. After a few minutes on the phone, I was shakily saying I thought I had a problem, and we agreed that she would escort me to a meeting of Alcoholics Anonymous. Unfortunately, it was not the meeting that would educate me into an understanding that I actually belonged in the club. In the basement of a Methodist church, I heard a man with wild eyes talk about the voices in his head. At that point, my alcohol-soaked brain didn't relate, and checked out. The next time it would check back in would be ten years later.

Manhattan to Florida 2005 — The 1st "geographic"

Living in Central Florida was one of the lowest periods of my life. It was the first of two times my husband and I moved in with my mom as adults. My soulmate, whom I had met at the circus, became my long-distance boyfriend, then fiancee, and we married in 2001 while living in Manhattan. Being a foreigner from a country that also didn't promote common education about alcoholism, he simply didn't understand what I was going through. I was very sneaky and very good at hiding how much I drank and glossing over the affects. So the abrupt job changes and moves I began orchestrating we thought were creative crises. Perhaps, but there was more going on. There is this thing known in recovery from alcoholism called a geographic. It occurs as a result of moving to another town, city, or country in the hopes of starting fresh. With reckless thinking, a person fantasizes that a new place will bring a new life. Opportunities, changes, chances. But in reality, the changed environment does not reflect a changed person. And who we were comes with us, for better. Or worse. During the five months of living at my mother's home, there was a lot of tension. Please keep in mind, a geographic move can happen for an alcoholic, whether they are drinking or not. If they aren't in recovery and working on their Spiritual self and personality, a person with alcoholism can engage in similar behaviors as they do while drinking. This is called being a dry drunk. Symptoms include; irritability, angry outbursts, manipulative behavior, mood swings, a tendency to lie, cheat, steal.... you name it. In February of 2007, we had been living at my mom's house for five months. It wasn't cozy. I think my mom was in complete fear that if she was soft and nurturing, we would never leave and become autonomous and independent. I also think that after years of living successfully by herself, she wasn't the type of personality to share a residence. We moved into an apartment in an outskirt village. My self-esteem plummeted lower than my finances, which was an extreme shock. My former salary of $65K in Manhattan became $6.50 per hour at The Hardrock players club, where I made cards as a customer service agent for gamblers. The bright light that God sent me during that disparaging time was Gina. (God always sends a bright light wherever you are — you've got to be smart enough to look for it and wise enough to connect with it). As I sat with her in the employee cafeteria bemoaning my fate and not understanding why what I WANTED hadn't come to pass, Gina turned me towards family matters. "You have so much love to give! If you want to have children, you should really consider starting now. Don't lose your chance."

Don't lose your chance. As fearful as I was to start a family, those words stuck with me. I knew what I had to do.

I hightailed it out of the smoky casino and got work for the US Postal Service. Living large at $12.63 per hour, ha! Though I wasn't willing to change my lifestyle (I showed up for work under the influence of marijuana a couple of times), a weird experience planted the seed that alcohol wasn't my friend.

One day, I was nearing the end of my shift at the postal center, a schedule which was ever changing and inconsistent. My mind had the thought of what the evening ahead would look like, and the nanosecond I THOUGHT of wine, an irritating, itchy red rash appeared on my body. Somehow, I knew they were connected, and yet I chose ignorance. In self-destructive defiance, I kept drinking. Par for the course, I kept changing jobs, hoping for a better work experience, better lifestyle, and to feel grounded and connected somewhere. Again, my creator blessed me with a lifeline — two local dance studios that taught adult ballet. I took classes irregularly, and never reached the feeling that I was liked, accepted, or made a real friend in the community. Of course, I felt that way because I didn't like myself at that time, but I kept blaming outside influences. The people in Florida were horrible. The weather was outrageously hot. The politics were weird. No one understood me. And on and on. I got on with a temporary employment agency and began working in offices, which felt more normal and comfortable for me, although I was working far below my talent level and capabilities. In October of 2007, exactly two years after moving to Florida, I abruptly stopped drinking alcohol and taking any substances other than multivitamins. My Earth angel's words rang in my ears: "Don't lose your chance." Consciously, I began to prepare for pregnancy.

The second week of February 2008, my childhood friends sent me a fertility kit. I knew it was time, as one of them aptly put it, "to take the plunge". Mid-cycle, on February 14th, I prayed to God during intimate time with my husband to bless us with a healthy baby. The next day, I stopped menstruating, and a month later, I had a positive pregnancy test. Words can never express the depth of my gratitude for those timely warnings and well-intentioned gifts of encouragement.

Florida to California 2007 — The second geographic

The first month of pregnancy produced one negative test after another. Down the road, a family pharmacist incited no small amount of embarrassment when I had purchased the 5th pregnancy test. He quasi muttered, "If I were your husband, I would just take you to the doctor." Like a person with an alcoholic mind, I couldn't even heed that advice. I simply started buying tests from CVS.

Upon pregnancy confirmation, I said to my husband, "I can't have our baby in this state. I must have our baby in my native home, in California." The power of a pregnant woman is underrated, and the Universe delivered. Within two weeks, my hubby had a job offer in Southern California, and we packed up our two-door Honda with Tordi, our English Bulldog that was his 30th birthday gift and headed back to my native home. I remember him saying, "Okay, I did this, now can we put down roots? No more moves, okay? This is it." As I nodded and happily smiled with a rush of conviction, looking back, I should have known better. But I couldn't have possibly — for I didn't know that while I wasn't drinking alcohol, I was living with an invisible disease. A disease that would never give me piece of mind and offered no reprieve from the state of anxiety. No, I still had a lot more humiliation and failure to endure before I received a suggestion that I might have a problem with alcohol, later confirmed by self inquiry.

Van Nuys to Chatsworth — The last geographic

As we pulled into the one-bedroom apartment with bars on the bedroom windows, I could not have anticipated that a realization would occur in that apartment. It was one that had been growing but lost in the demands of pregnancy, work, and education. We moved into that sublet in May of 2008, and it wasn't until several months after the birth of our first child in October of that year that I resumed drinking. Once I reintroduced it however, the potent combination of sleep deprivation, our son afflicted with severe colic, financial stress, breast feeding, hormones, and alcohol was an active Mt. Saint Helens. At this point, the doting energetic mom who I was – often at the park with our baby - took the lead upon waking until early evening. Somewhere imprinted in my consciousness was the belief that if I only drank at night, it was okay. I don't know where that came from. But it served as a fantastic justification for an ever-deluded personality that showed the external world one vision, felt very different internally, and drank away the difference. Consequences? No. I never drove while under the influence. A couple of times, I left our baby sleeping in the apartment by himself so I could drive up the street and buy wine while my husband was at work. *It never occurred to me that this wasn't normal.* In the back of my mind and heart, I knew that my behavior wasn't acceptable. I just chose to drink rather than think. And as such, developed a personality mechanism in which I projected who I desperately desired to be — and who I truly was on a soul level — a responsible, thoughtful, intelligent human being. On the other hand, emotional compensation for the loss of control, shame, discomfort, and frustration with my life was easy to achieve through three glasses to two bottles of wine once the sun went down. It was easy to mask while I was at home alone with my husband at work. Easy to cover with Ibuprofen and sunglasses. I drank not nightly, but episodically. More and more frequently, I thought, "I can't do this. I don't want to do this anymore." But those thoughts were drowned with part-time jobs, play dates, and a lot of bills we had trouble paying. This was one aspect of my life I had always struggled with. Money. There was never enough. It was always a huge pain point. And as an obliging person with an addiction, I wearily attempted to create and maintain wealth in between a precarious place of financial poverty and spiritual bankruptcy. One fateful night, my drinking caught up with me in hideous degradation when the gypsy woman who lived next door to our apartment asked me something about me being okay. Instantly, I had a flashback to the previous evening and a vague recollection of walking outside down to the sidewalk in my underwear. An internal line had been crossed, and I vowed that I would cleanse my body of toxins and not drink for 30 days. At the end of the 30 days, I said to my husband, "what if I didn't drink for an entire year?" He burst out laughing, and upon recognizing a wild determination in me, he said he thought that would be fine. A year went by, and I kept extending that time. And life slowly began to get better. In 2012, he took a trip back to his home of birth for a family visit and brought back enough cash from his savings for 6 months of rent in a better place. We found a shoddy rental home in a nice neighborhood of Chatsworth and began a new life with our young son. It felt like the greatest start. The middle class life that I had so desperately wanted and projected to our circle of family and friends actually started to materialize. Within months of moving into that new home with the big backyard, I integrated wine back into our nightly dinners. Within a couple of months, I was wasted three nights a week after dinner, and my life began to spin precariously out of control. This is a really important point: alcoholics will drink through bad times and good. Simultaneously I was holding down jobs, hiking with girlfriends, getting yoga and Reiki certificates and looking on the surface like a good suburban family member. The distance between who I was and who I projecting myself to be began to get wider and led me to make one of the biggest financial mistakes of my life, resulting in disastrous consequences. And I COULD NOT figure out why my friends my age were thriving, and why I felt like I could never get my life together, never access good luck, and never feel safe, secure, or successful. My mom offered to pay for therapy, and this is one of those life interventions for which I will never be able to fully express the gigantic amount of gratitude in my heart. Meeting Catherine set me on a path of healing that forever changed my life. Thank God I didn't know what was in store, for had I known how bad things would get, I may not have gotten on the sobriety train.

Chapter Two

2016 —
DISCOVERING
SOBRIETY

A psychotherapist & Spiritual program of recovery

After 30 minutes on the phone, my therapist said, "Well, you mentioned you have trouble eating well and sleeping after drinking alcohol. It seems like maybe you have a problem with that?" Being caught a bit off guard, I didn't have an opportunity to be defensive. This remembering is likely not verbatim, however I do know that she next said, "I want you to go to three AA meetings between now and our next session, and then you'll know." I ended up at a 6:45am 'Spiritual' meeting in Canoga Park. I had a reason to get dressed and put on my makeup. Sitting down, a man walked around with a basket and said if you have a card, put it in here. He stopped in front of me. "Where's your card?" I looked at him and said, "I don't have one!

Where do I get one of those?!" He laughed and moved on. Completely lacking understanding, my lifelong feeling of rejection and being an outsider swelled. It wasn't until years later that I understood that the man was collecting court cards for people who had to have proof of attendance at an AA meeting. There were high energy people with bright eyes. One of them called on me to share, and I broke down in tears confessing that it was my first meeting but I really felt like I belonged there. It was 2013, and technically my second AA meeting. Little did I know that when I came back to a meeting, it would be almost exactly two years later, the mom of a seven-year-old and nursing a 15 month-old baby.

Now here is a funky irony — in Alcoholics Anonymous, widely known and referred to as AA, there is a guideline about anonymity at the level of press, radio, and film. Clearly, a book counts as press. So what's the deal about this? Well, number 1. This is my story about recovery that I'm sharing to inspire others that they too, can get sober. Number 2. I'm not promoting A.A. I'm simply sharing that it's how I got sober. So there's that.

This phase of life proved not much different than others. Focusing on family, work, and education, some significant strides in my professional and educational development were made. I earned a variety of accredited alternative health certifications; children's yoga instructor, Reiki master, and Pranayama (breathwork) practitioner. I began taking online college classes with the intention of further progress on my associate's degree. Things seemed to be moving slowly and unsurely in a better direction. In the fall of 2013, my husband and I walked our son to his first day of TK and with tear-filled eyes admitted we were ready to bless him with a sibling. The next six months brought no small amount of pain as I poorly dealt with my last remaining grandmother's passing. In March of 2014, our dream came true, and in November, our second son was born. That happy period of our life was shadowed by my husband's job loss, and in 2015, we were both unemployed, arguing miserably, and trying to raise two vulnerable little beings caught in the throes of our chaotic dysfunctional household.

Karaoke to Calabasas

Thursday the 4th of February 2016. My mother-in-law was visiting us in our rented house in Chatsworth. She is from Moscow, and being a doting and understanding mother-in-law, she encouraged us to go out, celebrate life, and put fun time into our marriage. That was around 8:30pm. We returned several hours later, and I was wasted and enraged. I was screaming and proceeded to announce to her that her son did something so awful and so inappropriate that I wouldn't tell her because I didn't want to break her heart. Being the selfish and emotionally immature drunk that I was, I had already broken her heart and didn't stop along the way to notice. I am a blackout drunk, and most of the nights that I drank in my life, I cannot remember. Ironically, I remember that entire night. Every detail before, during, and after the glass of white wine, shot of vodka, and four long island ice teas. Had God parted the skies and told me in advance, "This will be the last time you consume alcohol in this lifetime," I would not have believed it. After an initially fun, sordid, and dramatic evening that ended with me driving our car while extremely drunk and attempting to punch my husband in the face, I went to bed — passed out rather. Somebody must have prayed. God must have had enough. Some conversion of the reckless woman to a repentant fool had occurred during the night, for I woke up and said with conviction to myself, "I can't do this anymore. I don't ever want to do that again." I looked up meetings for Alcoholics Anonymous and found a Friday night meeting. At 5:30pm that evening I walked in the doors and never ever looked back. Proverbially, of course!

Choose your mentors carefully – You'll get better results

The first months of sobriety were crazy. Money was practically nonexistent. With my husband employed part-time and me working odd jobs while caring for a 7 year old and infant, we were really stressed. Per usual. I remember showing him a website of an internet satellite company that was down the street from my mother's gorgeous forest home in Northern California and saying, "I can get a job there and we can live with my mom until we get on our feet." I went to meetings faithfully and kept up appearances, but my inner knowing must have sensed that life in L.A. was soon to expire. Regardless, I kept not drinking. To be honest, I didn't even have the desire to drink. I had the desire to live and figure things out. People approached me with a kind intention to be my sponsor, but I waited. This was the ONE time in my life in which I was patient and exceptionally choosy. I knew that to do this sobriety thing really well, I would need to work with other people, specifically women. During this period, in my deep quest for stability and security, I put into my head that I would become a nurse. I knew that it would give me the money we wanted and the stability I craved, so I set about looking for programs I could almost instantly enroll in. And I found such an opportunity in Loyola Marymount University. My mind was fixated on becoming an RN (fixation and impulsivity are common characteristics of alcoholism) and in May or June of 2016, I attended a woman's meeting in Woodland Hills. As I jumped into my car after the meeting, not bothering to hang out and commune with any of the people, my eye caught a license plate. "RN

♥ AA". I jumped out of my car and waited for the owner to arrive. When she walked up, I practically pounced on her and asked her to be my sponsor. The pretty and nice looking woman appeared slightly surprised and quickly surveyed me as if checking that I wasn't under the influence. It never occurred to me that I might appear that way, even if I wasn't, simply due to my big personality. She thoughtfully looked at me and steadily said that we could meet and talk about it. In the meantime, she suggested I could write about all of the things I wanted in a sponsor and some questions I might have for her. It was a novel idea, and I couldn't wait to get home and get started on my first assignment.

Little did I know, my Care Bear, as I affectionately called her, my very first sponsor, had the heart of a drill sergeant. She was NO JOKE and did not accept excuses. None. She assigned me the daunting task of attending 90 meetings in 90 days. I protested, big time; "I have two kids. I have multiple jobs. I'm trying to get into school." On and on were my lame attempts to not take the medicine. This is metaphorical, of course. In the world of recovery, for me personally, going to meetings and spending time with other alcoholics is medicine. Sometimes I am thrilled about the medicine, and other times I won't take it for weeks, even months. But eventually, a power greater than myself kicks my butt out of the excuses seat, and I go and participate in recovery life. This part I won't even dream about romanticizing, because that would leave you, the reader (and hopefully the person who needs motivation to take some form of Spiritual medicine in your life) thinking that the medicine is easy and fun. It CAN be. It CAN be. However, my experience is that in the beginning, it was hard. It was difficult waking up at 5am every day so that I could attend meetings and not adversely affect my family life. There were no meetings with childcare where I lived. It was hard and it was uncomfortable. And I did it. And it kept me sober.

Unfortunately, the medicine of meetings did not keep my life from falling apart. Let me paint you an analogy. When a person accepts Jeshua bin Joseph (commonly known as Jesus) into their life, they are not promised a life free of pain, fear, doubt, or hardships. They are promised Spiritual and heavenly assistance as they walk through all of the situations and lessons that life REQUIRES of us. Get that. WE ARE REQUIRED! No one is exempt. Within months of getting sober, my life quite literally started to fall apart. The professionally crafted website for my alternative healing practice was hacked and unable to be resurrected. My car died. But the biggest blow was an accident that my husband had in October of 2016. Our oldest son, in 2nd grade at the time, witnessed his dad's life changing accident that almost caused permanent disability. Physically wrecked and financially ruined, we were completely unable to cope with the demands of life while sustaining the injury with no medical support. After eight years of family life in Los Angeles, we packed our rental home within four weeks and moved to my mother's house in rural Northern California.

Starting life over in your early 40's is something that many people do in one way or another. They marry or divorce. Change careers. Travel out of their home country. Make a major move. Have a baby. Doing anything of those things in life naturally brings up fear and anxiety. Doing those things while newly sober is a whole different ballgame. Although I was a lucky woman because I had zero craving for alcohol, I didn't have any idea how to live my life better. I had to be vulnerable, ask questions, adopt modeling, and teach myself. Thankfully, I don't have a crystal ball, for if I had foreseen how difficult life would successively become, I might have thought about opting out.

After five months in my mom's forest escape, we needed to move our children to a bigger town with more community and better educational resources. As we did our entire life, we went where the work took us, and the work took us to Auburn. I dabbled in my medicine by finding a sponsor and attending meetings at the local fellowship. I began a government job working with children, a population similar to the awesome group of kiddos I taught yoga to in a private school in L.A. I was, however, wholly unprepared for the politics that accompany work in a non-private school setting — far from the 1099 employee I had been. Ten months later, I lost that position in a very political and humiliating manner. Panicked and poor, I quickly landed an entry level position at a senior living facility. As was the case with all of my job positions, I gained a reputation for working hard and being kind and reliable. This did not fit the motives of the disturbed human resources person, and in a shocking turn of events after witnessing a director commit a forgery of one of the residents, I was forced to resign. That happened five days after my husband suffered another life-changing injury that would take him out of work for two and a half years. I felt like Job of the bible. I cried out. I protested. I was in emotional turmoil and persistent anxiety. I did not understand what God was working in my life. Ever faithful, God led me to gainful employment at a non-profit that served people suffering from mental illness. And there began my foray into direct service work that I actually enjoyed and felt supported by the team I was on. The problem was $16.50. I made $16.50 an hour and with my husband out of work, we couldn't materially live on life's terms. I changed nonprofits two more times until I landed in a role that was similar to the work I had done early in my career in Manhattan. In the middle of the COVID-19 pandemic, I was stepping into a development career. My husband never fully healed from two failed surgeries, but he trudged on and went back to work. We squeaked by for a home loan and saved $12K for a down payment. We bought our first home by ourselves, without any help. The point here is that all of your problems don't go away when you stop drinking. You just actually start living in a manner that makes you fit to deal with them.

In the midst of all this, we, like most families on the planet, encountered innumerable changes. We changed schools, towns, jobs, and places of worship. I changed sponsors. We gained and lost pets. I finished an AA degree. In October of 2020, while taking a midterm for my astronomy class, my father passed away from Alzheimer's disease in Los Angeles. We had reconciled and enjoyed an easy relationship since 2008. Just writing this, it seems like life was overwhelming. And it was. But that overwhelm was tempered with beautiful moments. Our sons' academics. Hikes. Christmas. Another visit from my mother-in-law prior to my father-in-law's passing. Our oldest child discovered his exceptional talent for building computers and digital editing. Extended family and church community. Our youngest son emerged as incredibly talented in mountain biking and other sports. Visits to my mom's peaceful property and gatherings with friends. We experienced a very full life. All taking place in the midst of my sobriety.

I never counted the days; I just kept taking the medicine. I would go to meetings. Volunteer to take a commitment of some kind, whether it was being secretary of a meeting or speaking at a retreat. Many times I stayed on the fringe, but I also stayed in. Slowly, over the years, sobriety began to form the center of my being. It became an identity that I was proud to share. Being in recovery informed my creative life. I began to make alternative health videos again and started making use of my education and certifications; started teaching yoga and meditation to private clients. Sobriety inspired all of the ways I delved into entrepreneurialism though my alternative healing practice. My spirit was always thirsty for a mystical connection to the divine. Staying in the mundane world is difficult for creative types, and admittedly, I scattered a lot of energy. The most inefficient thing I did was allow myself to get pulled in a lot of different directions by competing interests. The best way I can sum this up is as follows; I wanted a homestead home-schooling housewife life with working as a choice. Rather, I signed up for multiple jobs while being under resourced, in addition to having problems with self-confidence and self-worth, plus a lack of focus type journey. Do you understand the challenge of envisioning the dream while living your reality? I think this is more common than is discussed in today's over saturated, over opinionated social media wars. Further complicating the issue for me was the abundance of the "new age/new consciousness prosperity gospel" that emphasized I deserved to be rich and materially wealthy and that if I just changed how I thought and took "inspired action" on the desires of my heart, that they would eventually come to pass. A la 'The Secret'. And perhaps it's absolutely true. Perhaps. Maybe I didn't do it right, long enough, or well enough. But for whatever reasons, the material manifestation didn't work for me to the extent that I ever felt truly well, supported, abundant, and free. Financial insecurity worry always weighed me and my family down. Our kids were born into and indoctrinated into that. And we've worked so hard to reverse it, but it's a persistent challenge. It is an aspect of my work that I call financial sobriety. Meant to teach us several things: 1. The value of work 2. The importance of self-discipline and delayed gratification 3. How to be a good steward of our resources 4. Putting people before money 5. Learning ultimately to trust a benevolent God.

With all of this learning underway, again, I couldn't have imagined what was coming for me in Spring of 2024. Timing is so much of life, and when the timing is right (and even when it's not) when either you or the Divine decide that it's time for you to heal, it's time. You will have to undertake this process, and if there's resistance, it only creates more challenge and pain, in my humble opinion. So it happened like this. I had just landed a fabulous position working for a prestigious nonprofit at the Capitol. Although I initially had some reservations about the role, I blew right past them because the money was right, and I was excited to work with people face to face. After having worked remotely for two years, I realized that didn't fit my personality nor optimize my talent. So, I began shortly after the New Year what I would have called a "dream job." Simultaneously, I was called to explore shadow work. My Spirit was calling me to address some deep hidden guilt that I had been storing. The reason that this is so important is because it was deep work. It took me back to my drinking and pre-drinking life: to bad choices and decisions I made, based on a trauma response in my body. I was steeped in shame and regret and was dragged through a journey of responsibility and release. At times, my personal development was thoughtful and methodical. Like a creative writing scientist, I would create prompts for myself and journal. Once, I took the medicine by going to a meeting and I gravitated toward a woman who had some similar experiences to me. I spoke with her after the meeting, blurting out things I had done and what I was afraid of, and she gave me a reassuring smile. "You will know what to do. It will be okay!" I so deeply wanted to believe her. Most days, I was beset by stomach quivers and an aching heart. I developed migraines almost daily. And my fabulous new career job that I was so proud of wasn't shaping up to be the experience I had imagined it to be. Really, Universe. REALLY? There wasn't extra money for therapy, and I didn't have insurance that covered mental health services. I doggedly pursued healing. Volunteering. Focusing on my family and our pets. Waking up and praying, asking to be more grateful and of higher service. Begging God to put the past behind me and relieve me of the bondage of my sins. Please don't be freaked out by the word sin. Sin simply means turning away from God. We all know (or should know) what the seven sins and the ten commandments are. If you don't, please look them up. I fashion myself and my life around them. You don't have to, but familiarize yourself with them. You won't be sorry or regret that you did.

Chapter Three

MEETING LILITH AND BLOSSOMING MARY

Meeting Lilith

While sitting in church one day in either late 2023 or early 2024, I wondered inside of my head what I needed to heal. What must I do to start to achieve consistent happiness and familial and career success? While the associate pastor started to talk about upcoming events, I asked God, "What do I need to know in this moment?" Picking up the bible, I took a deep conscious breath while turning to a passage. God clearly meant for me to have that passage, in that moment. Since then, I have looked for those same words repeatedly, always failing. The feeling that came over my body as I read the small black typed words — it was a recognition of not only something I had done wrong, but a whole aspect of my being that I hadn't wanted to see. The shadow. It was nothing less than serendipitous that about a week later, I was online looking for mystical clues that would lead me to healing. I believed strongly in the power of Jesus Christ, of the Saints, Angels, Mystics, and Sages that had transformed more significant grievances. I revisited the Upanishads, Autobiography of a Yogi, The Diamond that Cuts through Illusion — all of the sacred ancient texts from across the world that I had first dove into while suffering through my early 20's. With my Spiritual fire reinvigorated, I consumed vast amounts of information with intermittent stillness.

While diving into this journey of self, I met Kristin, an alternative healer who helps people based on their birthday. She is the woman that opened the door for me to understand that I needed to do shadow work. She taught me about a concept called the Black Moon Lilith. I didn't and still don't see it as an astrological concept. I understand Lilith as a biblical or Spiritual character that has endured a variety of interpretations. My best interpretation of her is as an archetype of a wounded woman who went astray in life through alcoholism. She was redeemed by Jesus who restored her birth name of Mary. And when I learned about Lilith, it slowly dawned on me. I had the light of realization that I was undergoing an archetypal transformation from the person I was to the person I was meant to be. A light bulb clicked on, and I said to Kristin, "I am going from Lilith to Mary." Mary as in the symbolic Mother Mary. Relax, folks, I was not thinking that I was becoming the mother to Christ. I just began to understand that the quest to be the best human being I can be feels very aligned with the sacred heart of Mother Mary; filled with wisdom, grace, and endless unconditional love. Through that instant discovery, this book was born.

The impetus to embrace the qualities of Mother Mary is noble — and difficult. No sooner do I transmute some negative energy of toxic memory, and I am gifted with an opportunity to forgive, forget, and step into a deeper layer of unconditional love.

It's not easy, or at least it doesn't feel that way. One to one hundred times per day, I breathe deeply, bite my tongue, and rearrange a judgmental thought. My every morning and late nights are prayer filled. Always, I'm asking God/The Universe/Sacred Creation/My Higher Power to please do five things:

#1 Bless all human beings, all eight billion of us on this planet, to have and hold our Spiritual connection and sovereignty with God.

#2 Provide all human beings with safety in their body, mind, heart, and soul.

#3 Provide all human beings with free access to fresh clean abundant water.

#4 Give all human beings affordable access to healthy nutrient dense fresh food.

#5 Bless all people on Earth with a safe and comfortable home.

It might seem simple and trite on the surface, but you can imagine all people with these basic needs met, how many violent stress responses it will heal.

In my mind, this thinking embraces the compassion that flows from the heart of the great mothers. Mother Mary and Mother Earth. They support, shield, provide, and guide. They protect, shelter, feed, water, and nourish us. Our own consciousness craves recognition of our providers. This is the essence of gratitude. What my journey to Mary has taught me is that no one can determine my destiny or tell my story. Our lives are constructed to bring us to the brink — all of the things that can become a barrier to our path of progress are actually designed to help us find our inner light and find and strengthen our relationship with God. It is very basic and extremely challenging. The acceleration of our Spiritual progress is in direct proportion to our willingness to be in relationship with God. We pray for guidance. Take action. And surrender the results. That's it! If every there was a formula for the Spiritual life, that is an All-In-One; Pray, Do, Rest. Friends, I urge you to identify one thing you wish you could change or improve in your life. Whatever aspect you have control over, exercise that control and do your best to help your dream come alive.

The Present Moment

At the time of this writing, I am inhabiting and preparing for a lot of newness. My life is in a constant state of multilayered movement. My husband and I are preparing our home to be put on the market to sell. We are searching for a more aligned home with fervent hope that our prayers will be answered. We have one child preparing his list of Universities he wants to apply for in the upcoming school year. Our younger son is changing schools and sports. I've recently joined my fourth non-profit as an Associate Director and struggle to find time for the homework required for the University program I started this year in pursuit of my bachelor's. Yet, in all of that the true goals remain the same. I am thankful for happiness with family and being a valued community contributor.

Whatever you wish to change in your life, you can, and you will. It takes soul-baring honesty. Often, alcoholism in particular shows up as a mixture of shame, fear, anxiety, and guilt. This toxicity can be transmuted into calmness and self-compassion. I wish this for you, and the ultimate truth is that you have to want it for yourself. It's uncomfortable work, requiring diligence and grit. But you can do it. You CAN.

I felt called to write this for you because you need to know that you are not alone. Shame is a room you don't have to live in. You can and will forgive yourself. God has already forgiven you; if you want proof, just ask. Faith will pay you back exponentially. Show one ounce of faith, and you will receive hundred thousand ounces of unconditional love. You are worthy to be your best self and live the highest potential of this lifetime. You are worthy of love. You will make it. It's your destiny, even if no one ever told you that before.

That's it. That's all I wanted to share with you. A little story, a lot of love, and prayerfully a dose of wisdom.

I invite and encourage you to ask yourself; What's your medicine? Are you willing to take it? If not, why? If you take it, what will you lose? If you take it, what will you gain? What might happen if you don't take it at all?

I love you. I am praying for you.

From the sacred heart of Mother Mary to yours!

Love, Tai